Journaling Workbook

Comparison Girl

Lessons *from* Jesus *on* Me-Free Living *in a* Measure-Up World

SHANNON POPKIN

KREGEL
PUBLICATIONS

Author is represented by the literary agency of Credo Communications, LLC, Grand Rapids, Michigan, www.credocommunications.net.

ISBN 978-0-8254-4703-7

Printed in the United States of America

21 22 23 24 25 26 27 28 29 30 / 5 4 3 2 1

Contents

Welcome!

Dear Friend,

Thanks for being my companion as we travel with Jesus through *Comparison Girl* over the next six weeks or so. My hope for this journaling workbook is to give you a place to take a minute to process what the Lord is teaching you and to record your responses, plans, and commitments.

As Comparison Girls, we have a lot to think through. Most of us stumble into comparison thinking only of ourselves—oblivious to the enemy who keeps pressing us to prove we measure up, then shaming us when we don't. But if we're going to leave the bondage and isolation of this measure-up mindset, we've got to start listening to the voice of Jesus, not our enemy. This journaling workbook is the place to do exactly that.

Jesus never taught us not to compare. He just taught us a different *way* to compare. He constantly wove his red-letter comparisons into conversations and stories, reminding us, "The greatest among you shall be your servant. The last will be first, and the first last. Whoever exalts herself will be humbled, and whoever humbles herself will be exalted" (see Matt. 20:16; 23:11–12). These red-letter comparisons of Jesus are what guard us against our enemy when he comes whispering messages like, "Look at her . . . Compared to her, you're worthless." If we've listened long and hard enough to the voice of Jesus, we know enough to say, "Yeah, that's the voice of my enemy. Jesus wouldn't say that."

So, are you ready? Do you have your red pen poised, ready to underline the words of Jesus? Are you ready to be one of the sheep who knows his voice? I'm so excited to be your study companion as we learn to listen and follow Jesus together.

Warmly,

What's Included

This journaling workbook is meant to offer you extra support as you work through *Comparison Girl*, either on your own or with a group. If you are using this workbook to lead a group study, please visit ComparisonGirl.com for a free leader's guide. Below are the features included in your journaling workbook:

- *Meditation.* At the end of each lesson in *Comparison Girl* is a "For Meditation" section. This workbook provides space to reflect on and write out the Scripture verse and meditation on that lesson's truth. Studies show that writing by hand helps us more deeply understand and remember.* That's the goal, right?

- *Responses to questions.* Also following each lesson in the book are some questions that provide additional Bible verses and ways to apply what you're learning. Yes, you could probably just answer in your head, but writing your responses will slow you down and help your heart reflect and receive truth.

- *"Living by the Spout" journal prompts.* In this workbook, I share lots of additional stories, plus a few recapped ones from the book and the video sessions, inviting you to respond with reflective journaling. May these pages help you process your past and bring clarity to the next steps of your journey.

- *Video session responses.* The video sessions are designed to correlate with each of the six chapters in *Comparison Girl*. In this workbook, I've included space for you to take notes on these sessions.

---

* Jennifer Fink, "The Case for Handwriting," Scholastic, accessed September 25, 2020, https://www.scholastic.com/teachers/articles/teaching-content/case-handwriting/.

- *Bible study and discussion.* This feature includes the Scripture verses I teach from in the video sessions. Follow along with the verses as you watch the video, then work through the discussion questions, ideally with a group. The workbook provides three additional versions of the passages so you can compare translations. The first version is double-spaced, offering you extra room to mark your observations.

- *Extras.* I've included some extra quotes and verses for you to reflect on.

- *Introduction and conclusion.* Begin your study by processing your starting place, and finish by recording what you've learned and where you're headed.

I'm so excited to get started with you! Let's make the most of this time together and learn all we can from our Lord Jesus as he shares lessons on me-free living in a measure-up world.

Introduction

The Makings of a Comparison Girl

Record your "Comparison Girl starting point" thoughts from pages 23–24 of *Comparison Girl*.

Do You Want to Be Free?

Comparison leads us into bondage. Which part of me-free living listed on page 22 do you most want to experience?

I want to be free _____.

Which of these red-letter comparisons from Jesus do you think might lead to the freedom you long for?

"The person who exalts herself will be humbled, but the person who humbles herself will be exalted" (see Luke 18:14).

"Many who are first will be last, and the last first" (Matt. 19:30).

"Whoever exalts herself will be humbled, and whoever humbles herself will be exalted" (see Matt. 23:12).

"So the last will be first, and the first last" (Matt 20:16).

"If anyone would be first, [she] must be last of all and servant of all" (Mark 9:35).

"Whoever would be first among you must be your slave, even as the Son of Man came not to be served but to serve" (Matt. 20:27–28).

"The greatest among you shall be your servant" (Matt. 23:11).

"Let the greatest among you become as the youngest, and the leader as one who serves" (Luke 22:26).

On the following page, rewrite the red-letter comparison that you most want to remember. Perhaps you'll want to use a red pen.

Chapter 1

From Measuring Up to Pouring Out

Red-Letter Comparison

*The Son of Man came not to be served
but to serve.*

—Matthew 20:28

Lesson 1

The Lines or the Spout

Write out the verse and meditation from page 33:

....

....

....

....

....

....

....

Record your responses to the questions on page 33:

....

....

....

....

....

....

....

....

....

....

....

....

Satan points to the lines; King Jesus points to the spout.

—*Comparison Girl*, page 31

[Jesus] emptied himself, by taking the form of a servant.

—Philippians 2:7

Living by the Spout

As a successful thirtysomething, my friend Sarah was preoccupied with her looks, her accomplishments, and her silver Mercedes—the biggest one they made. Sarah cussed like a sailor and had no problem gossiping about others, and most weeks she emptied several bottles of wine on her own. She was materialistic, superficial, worldly, and opinionated. Though Sarah had grown up knowing Jesus, she had little room for him now that the measure-up ways of the world consumed her life. Yet somehow this caused her regret.

Sarah was out for lunch one day and told her friend through tears that she wished she could give her life back to God, but she didn't see how it was possible. Her lifestyle had created too many obstacles. "Too much would have to change," she said.

Can you relate to Sarah? What would have to change if you were to reject the measure-up ways of this world? Record your thoughts in the space below.

In some respects, Sarah had the right idea when she said, "Too much would have to change." The notion that it costs something to become a follower of Jesus is one that came from Jesus himself. Jesus completely emptied his measuring cup, and he wants his followers to do the same—either in once-for-all or bits-at-a-time ways. But those who determine Jesus is worth it are the ones who look beyond the sky's blue veil and see the glitter of the life to come.

Just a few months after the lunch date with her friend, Sarah was invited to a church service, and at the end she went forward and emptied out her life on the altar before God. She was so done, tired of chasing the measure-up rewards of the world. She wanted Jesus, and she decided he was worth it. That day, Sarah lost her life and found it (Matt. 10:39).

From that day on, Sarah's lifestyle shifted dramatically. She began loving her husband, cherishing her daughter, and serving her family—not herself. Her calendar filled with Bible study, prayer, and fellowship with other believers. She began denying herself and saying yes to God. Today, when Sarah puts her old life next to her new one, it's as if she's lost nothing. She's found Jesus! She's gained the kingdom. And the rewards of this world do not compare.

Can you think of any pivotal moments when you made the choice to stop chasing the measure-up rewards of the world? What prompted this? How have things turned out?

When was the last time you—like Sarah—surrendered your life ambitions before God? How have you "lost your life to find it" (see Matt. 10:39)? If you never have, will you set aside time with Jesus to surrender your life to his plans for you today? Who will you contact to talk this through?

Our jealousy and selfish ambition serve as "Satan was here" graffiti on the walls of our lives.

—Comparison Girl, page 35

Lesson 2

Green-Eyed Wisdom

The verses from pages 34–35 are reprinted below, if you'd prefer to mark them here.

> If your heart is one that bleeds dark streams of (jealousy) and selfish-
> ness, do not be so proud that you ignore your depraved state. The
> wisdom of this world should never be mistaken for heavenly wisdom;
> it originates below in the earthly realms, with the demons. Any place
> where you find jealousy and selfish ambition, you will discover chaos
> and evil thriving under its rule. (James 3:14–16 VOICE)

Write out the verse and meditation from page 39:

But if you have bitter jealously and selfish ambition in your hearts ... this is not the wisdom that comes down from above. James 3:14-15

Record your responses to the questions on page 39:

Lesson 3

Pride-Thickened Comparison Walls

Write out the verse and meditation from pages 46–47:

....

....

....

....

....

Record your responses to the questions on page 46:

....

....

....

....

....

....

....

....

....

....

Pride thickens our comparison walls, but humility collapses them.

—*Comparison Girl,*
page 44

Lesson 4

A Rival Named Jesus

Write out the verse and meditation from page 54:

_____

_____

_____

_____

_____

_____

_____

Record your responses to the questions on page 54:

_____

_____

_____

_____

_____

_____

_____

_____

_____

_____

_____

Trying to solve
the problem of
self-focus with more
self-focus
isn't helping.
It's making
things worse.

—Comparison Girl,
page 52

Lesson 5

A Place to Belong

Write out the verse and meditation from pages 62–63:

....

....

....

....

....

....

Record your responses to the questions on page 62:

....

....

....

....

....

....

....

....

....

....

....

....

....

....

Living by the Spout

As a pastor's wife, Jane felt like Facebook was becoming a full-time job. She was working so hard to keep track of the needs, prayer requests, and celebrations of all "her people"—making sure they saw that she saw what they had posted. She labored over her comments— trying to sound spiritual enough, yet lighthearted and fun.

Jane was trying so hard to give equal attention, but then she posted a photo of her family out on a boat with another family from church and got a phone call from a woman in tears whose family hadn't been included. Jane felt she couldn't win.

What pressure do you feel from the people you know who are comparing and measuring on social media?

Which of your relationships are tainted because of measure-up comparing online? How about in person? How have you reacted to the pressure you feel? How do you think Jesus is calling you to respond?

Video Session 1

Notes

_____

_____

_____

_____

_____

_____

_____

_____

_____

_____

_____

_____

_____

_____

_____

_____

_____

_____

_____

_____

_____

_____

_____

_____

_____

Bible Study and Discussion

Take some time to study the Bible passage I taught from in the video session. The questions below will help you make observations about the text (on the next page) and discuss what you're learning. Mark repeated words, correlating ideas, conjunction words, and other notable features. The additional Bible versions on the following pages can aid in your observations as you notice different word choices.

- Contrast the different voices mentioned. What was Jesus teaching?

- Contrast the shepherd and the thief/wolf. What warning was Jesus giving?

- What are the wolf's tactics? What can we learn about protecting ourselves?

- Look at the contrast in verses 12 and 16 between scattering and gathering. How does comparison, in particular, prompt scattering rather than gathering?

John 10:1–16

"Truly, truly, I say to you, he who does not enter the sheepfold by the door but climbs in by another way, that man is a thief and a robber. But he who enters by the door is the shepherd of the sheep. To him the gatekeeper opens. The sheep hear his voice, and he calls his own sheep by name and leads them out. When he has brought out all his own, he goes before them, and the sheep follow him, for they know his voice. A stranger they will not follow, but they will flee from him, for they do not know the voice of strangers." This figure of speech Jesus used with them, but they did not understand what he was saying to them.

So Jesus again said to them, "Truly, truly, I say to you, I am the door of the sheep. All who came before me are thieves and robbers, but the sheep did not listen to them. I am the door. If anyone enters by me, he will be saved and will go in and out and find pasture. The thief comes only to steal and kill and destroy. I came that they may have life and have it abundantly. I am the good shepherd. The good shepherd lays down his life for the sheep. He who is a hired hand and not a shepherd, who does not own the sheep, sees the wolf coming and leaves the sheep and flees, and the wolf snatches them and scatters them. He flees because he is a hired hand and cares nothing for the sheep. I am the good shepherd. I know my own and my own know me, just as the Father knows me and I know the Father; and I lay down my life for the sheep. And I have other sheep that are not of this fold. I must bring them also, and they will listen to my voice. So there will be one flock, one shepherd."

John 10:1–16 NIV

"Very truly I tell you Pharisees, anyone who does not enter the sheep pen by the gate, but climbs in by some other way, is a thief and a robber. The one who enters by the gate is the shepherd of the sheep. The gatekeeper opens the gate for him, and the sheep listen to his voice. He calls his own sheep by name and leads them out. When he has brought out all his own, he goes on ahead of them, and his sheep follow him because they know his voice. But they will never follow a stranger; in fact, they will run away from him because they do not recognize a stranger's voice." Jesus used this figure of speech, but the Pharisees did not understand what he was telling them.

Therefore Jesus said again, "Very truly I tell you, I am the gate for the sheep. All who have come before me are thieves and robbers, but the sheep have not listened to them. I am the gate; whoever enters through me will be saved. They will come in and go out, and find pasture. The thief comes only to steal and kill and destroy; I have come that they may have life, and have it to the full.

"I am the good shepherd. The good shepherd lays down his life for the sheep. The hired hand is not the shepherd and does not own the sheep. So when he sees the wolf coming, he abandons the sheep and runs away. Then the wolf attacks the flock and scatters it. The man runs away because he is a hired hand and cares nothing for the sheep.

"I am the good shepherd; I know my sheep and my sheep know me—just as the Father knows me and I know the Father—and I lay down my life for the sheep. I have other sheep that are not of this sheep pen. I must bring them also. They too will listen to my voice, and there shall be one flock and one shepherd."

John 10:1–16 NLT

"I tell you the truth, anyone who sneaks over the wall of a sheepfold, rather than going through the gate, must surely be a thief and a robber! But the one who enters through the gate is the shepherd of the sheep. The gatekeeper opens the gate for him, and the sheep recognize his voice and come to him. He calls his own sheep by name and leads them out. After he has gathered his own flock, he walks ahead of them, and they follow him because they know his voice. They won't follow a stranger; they will run from him because they don't know his voice."

Those who heard Jesus use this illustration didn't understand what he meant, so he explained it to them: "I tell you the truth, I am the gate for the sheep. All who came before me were thieves and robbers. But the true sheep did not listen to them. Yes, I am the gate. Those who come in through me will be saved. They will come and go freely and will find good pastures. The thief's purpose is to steal and kill and destroy. My purpose is to give them a rich and satisfying life.

"I am the good shepherd. The good shepherd sacrifices his life for the sheep. A hired hand will run when he sees a wolf coming. He will abandon the sheep because they don't belong to him and he isn't their shepherd. And so the wolf attacks them and scatters the flock. The hired hand runs away because he's working only for the money and doesn't really care about the sheep.

"I am the good shepherd; I know my own sheep, and they know me, just as my Father knows me and I know the Father. So I sacrifice my life for the sheep. I have other sheep, too, that are not in this sheepfold. I must bring them also. They will listen to my voice, and there will be one flock with one shepherd."

John 10:1–16 VOICE

Jesus: I tell you the truth: the man who crawls through the fence of the sheep pen, rather than walking through the gate, is a thief or a vandal. The shepherd walks openly through the entrance. The guard who is posted to protect the sheep opens the gate for the shepherd, and the sheep hear his voice. He calls his own sheep by name and leads them out. When all the sheep have been gathered, he walks on ahead of them; and they follow him because they know his voice. The sheep would not be willing to follow a stranger; they run because they do not know the voice of a stranger.

Jesus explained a profound truth through this metaphor, but they did not understand His teaching. So He explained further.

Jesus: I tell you the truth: I am the gate of the sheep. All who approached the sheep before Me came as thieves and robbers, and the sheep did not listen to their voices. I am the gate; whoever enters through Me will be liberated, will go in and go out, and will find pastures. The thief approaches with malicious intent, looking to steal, slaughter, and destroy; I came to give life with joy and abundance.

I am the good shepherd. The good shepherd lays down His life for the sheep in His care. The hired hand is not like the shepherd caring for His own sheep. When a wolf attacks, snatching and scattering the sheep, he runs for his life, leaving them defenseless. The hired hand runs because he works only for wages and does not care for the sheep. I am the good shepherd; I know My sheep, and My sheep know Me. As the Father knows Me, I know the Father; I will give My life for the sheep. There are many more sheep than you can see here, and I will bring them as well. They will hear My voice, and the flock will be united. One flock. One shepherd.

Chapter 2

Comparing Your Sin and Mine

Red-Letter Comparison

The person who exalts herself will be humbled, but the person who humbles herself will be exalted.

—Luke 18:14 (paraphrase)

Lesson 1

Sideways Disgust

Write out the verse and meditation from page 73:

Record your responses to the questions on pages 72–73:

Living by the Spout

When Mandy picked her kids up from school, her son, Jake—leaning over to rifle through the grocery bags—asked, "Did you get us anything good at the store, Mom?" Just then, he spotted the sparkling juice in its pretty foil wrapper. "Oooohhh! Can we have this stuff, Mom?"

Mandy explained that no, the sparkling juice was a treat for the grown-ups, but she had gotten the kids some fruit punch. "We never get the good stuff," Jake complained. "We just get *punch*." He punched the seat for emphasis. A moment later, Jake's little sister began singing sweetly, "Be thankful . . . be thankful . . ." She concocted a whole song about being thankful for fruit punch. But Jake was not impressed. "Why do you think it's your job to always make me feel like the worst Christian ever?" he snarled.

Is there someone who makes you feel like the "worst Christian ever"? What do they say or do to trigger your sense of frustration and inadequacy? How do you usually respond?

To renew your mind, write a short summary of God's plan for cleaning up your sin. How will you choose to trust God with your "worst Christian ever" feelings of inadequacy?

Lesson 2

An Empty Courtroom

Write out the verse and meditation from page 81:

_____

_____

_____

_____

_____

_____

Record your responses to the questions on pages 80–81:

_____

_____

_____

_____

_____

_____

_____

_____

_____

_____

_____

_____

Living by the Spout

Candice was twenty, single, and expecting a baby—and she was all alone. In response to this news, Candice's friends and family didn't offer love and support; instead, they pulled away. Candice felt like in every room she walked into, people were looking down on her, so she retreated to isolation—which is exactly what Satan wanted.

Candice fell into a deep depression. Even getting out of bed in the morning was hard. The enemy pummeled her with messages like, "You're not good enough. You're a disaster. You'll never amount to anything. You're not worth it."

Thankfully, Candice found respite in a loving and supportive church. She joined a Bible study group. She went to counseling and got help. Candice is now a single mom who follows Jesus alongside other believers.

Picture yourself walking into the various "rooms" of your life—family, friends, neighborhood, church, and so on. In which room do you feel looked down upon? By whom? What steps have you taken to pull away as a result?

What lies does the enemy come at you with in isolation? What steps do you need to take to find Christian support and community?

Lesson 3

God's Chair Is Off-Limits

Write out the verse and meditation from page 89:

....

....

....

....

....

Record your responses to the questions on pages 88–89:

....

....

....

....

....

....

....

....

....

....

....

Let's be careful
not to judge others
because they sin
differently than
we do.

—Cindy Bultema
Comparison Girl,
page 85

Lesson 4

Flipping My Ruler

Write out the verse and meditation from page 96:

....

....

....

....

....

....

....

Record your responses to the questions on pages 95–96:

....

....

....

....

....

....

....

....

....

....

....

....

Living by the Spout

Growing up, Renee didn't have a good relationship with her dad. She never felt loved or accepted by him, and that's one of the reasons she has treasured the close relationships with everyone in her husband's family. Everyone, that is, except for her sister-in-law Beth.

When I asked Renee why Beth grates on her so, she thought for a moment and said, "I think it started early on when I noticed the way she takes for granted her dad's affection." Beth is completely dismissive when her dad gives her a hug. She brushes him aside when he says, "Love you, hon!" To Renee, this is appalling. She would *love* the gift of an attentive, loving father. And so for years now, she's been measuring Beth's dismissiveness by the millimeter. But as Renee weighs and calculates every little sign of Beth's ungratefulness, the disgust in her own heart grows.

Who in your life has something you don't, but takes it for granted? What signs do you see?

How do you feel about her ingratitude? How would you finish the following sentence? "I would never _____." How do you see your own sin of contempt growing as you measure her sin?

Video Session 2

Notes

Bible Study and Discussion

Take some time to study the Bible passage I taught from in the video session. The questions below will help you make observations about the text (on the next page) and discuss what you're learning. Mark repeated words, correlating ideas, conjunction words, and other notable features. The additional Bible versions on the following pages can aid in your observations as you notice different word choices.

- Look for comparison words like *more* and *less* and *larger*. What is being compared?

- Contrast Simon's reaction to Jesus with the woman's. What do you learn about their hearts?

- Contrast the woman's way of honoring Jesus with Simon's. What do you learn about their hearts?

- What story does Jesus tell? What might a one-debtor version of the story be? Why does Jesus put two characters into his story?

- How are the two characters in Jesus's "story problem" similar and different? How is Jesus using this story problem to compare something in the real-life scenario before him?

- How does Jesus compare the foot washing, kiss, and ointment given by the woman with those given by Simon? Why do you think Jesus called these out?

- Which character do you see yourself in? Simon? The woman?

Luke 7:36–50

One of the Pharisees asked him to eat with him, and he went into the Pharisee's house and reclined at table. And behold, a woman of the city, who was a sinner, when she learned that he was reclining at table in the Pharisee's house, brought an alabaster flask of ointment, and standing behind him at his feet, weeping, she began to wet his feet with her tears and wiped them with the hair of her head and kissed his feet and anointed them with the ointment. Now when the Pharisee who had invited him saw this, he said to himself, "If this man were a prophet, he would have known who and what sort of woman this is who is touching him, for she is a sinner." And Jesus answering said to him, "Simon, I have something to say to you." And he answered, "Say it, Teacher."

"A certain moneylender had two debtors. One owed five hundred denarii, and the other fifty. When they could not pay, he cancelled the debt of both. Now which of them will love him more?" Simon answered, "The one, I suppose, for whom he cancelled the larger debt." And he said to him, "You have judged rightly." Then turning toward the woman he said to Simon, "Do you see this woman? I entered your house; you gave me no water for my feet, but she has wet my feet with her tears and wiped them with her hair. You gave me no kiss, but from the time I came in she has not ceased to kiss my feet. You did not anoint my head with oil, but she has anointed my feet with ointment. Therefore I tell you, her sins, which are many, are forgiven—for she loved much. But he who is forgiven little, loves little." And he said to her, "Your sins are forgiven." Then those who were at table with him began to say among themselves, "Who is this, who even forgives sins?" And he said to the woman, "Your faith has saved you; go in peace."

Luke 7:36–50 NIV

When one of the Pharisees invited Jesus to have dinner with him, he went to the Pharisee's house and reclined at the table. A woman in that town who lived a sinful life learned that Jesus was eating at the Pharisee's house, so she came there with an alabaster jar of perfume. As she stood behind him at his feet weeping, she began to wet his feet with her tears. Then she wiped them with her hair, kissed them and poured perfume on them.

When the Pharisee who had invited him saw this, he said to himself, "If this man were a prophet, he would know who is touching him and what kind of woman she is—that she is a sinner."

Jesus answered him, "Simon, I have something to tell you."

"Tell me, teacher," he said.

"Two people owed money to a certain moneylender. One owed him five hundred denarii, and the other fifty. Neither of them had the money to pay him back, so he forgave the debts of both. Now which of them will love him more?"

Simon replied, "I suppose the one who had the bigger debt forgiven."

"You have judged correctly," Jesus said.

Then he turned toward the woman and said to Simon, "Do you see this woman? I came into your house. You did not give me any water for my feet, but she wet my feet with her tears and wiped them with her hair. You did not give me a kiss, but this woman, from the time I entered, has not stopped kissing my feet. You did not put oil on my head, but she has poured perfume on my feet. Therefore, I tell you, her many sins have been forgiven—as her great love has shown. But whoever has been forgiven little loves little."

Then Jesus said to her, "Your sins are forgiven."

The other guests began to say among themselves, "Who is this who even forgives sins?"

Jesus said to the woman, "Your faith has saved you; go in peace."

Luke 7:36–50 NLT

One of the Pharisees asked Jesus to have dinner with him, so Jesus went to his home and sat down to eat. When a certain immoral woman from that city heard he was eating there, she brought a beautiful alabaster jar filled with expensive perfume. Then she knelt behind him at his feet, weeping. Her tears fell on his feet, and she wiped them off with her hair. Then she kept kissing his feet and putting perfume on them.

When the Pharisee who had invited him saw this, he said to himself, "If this man were a prophet, he would know what kind of woman is touching him. She's a sinner!"

Then Jesus answered his thoughts. "Simon," he said to the Pharisee, "I have something to say to you."

"Go ahead, Teacher," Simon replied.

Then Jesus told him this story: "A man loaned money to two people—500 pieces of silver to one and 50 pieces to the other. But neither of them could repay him, so he kindly forgave them both, canceling their debts. Who do you suppose loved him more after that?"

Simon answered, "I suppose the one for whom he canceled the larger debt."

"That's right," Jesus said. Then he turned to the woman and said to Simon, "Look at this woman kneeling here. When I entered your home, you didn't offer me water to wash the dust from my feet, but she has washed them with her tears and wiped them with her hair. You didn't greet me with a kiss, but from the time I first came in, she has not stopped kissing my feet. You neglected the courtesy of olive oil to anoint my head, but she has anointed my feet with rare perfume.

"I tell you, her sins—and they are many—have been forgiven, so she has shown me much love. But a person who is forgiven little shows only little love." Then Jesus said to the woman, "Your sins are forgiven."

The men at the table said among themselves, "Who is this man, that he goes around forgiving sins?"

And Jesus said to the woman, "Your faith has saved you; go in peace."

Luke 7:36–50 VOICE

Once a Pharisee named Simon invited Jesus to be a guest for a meal.

Picture this:

Just as Jesus enters the man's home and takes His place at the table, a woman from the city—notorious as a woman of ill repute—follows Him in. She has heard that Jesus will be at the Pharisee's home, so she comes in and approaches Him, carrying an alabaster flask of perfumed oil. Then she begins to cry, she kneels down so her tears fall on Jesus' feet, and she starts wiping His feet with her own hair. Then she actually kisses His feet, and she pours the perfumed oil on them.

Simon *(thinking)*: Now I know this guy is a fraud. If He were a real prophet, He would have known this woman is a sinner and He would never let her get near Him, much less touch Him . . . or kiss Him!

Jesus *(knowing what the Pharisee is thinking)*: Simon, I want to tell you a story.

Simon: Tell me, Teacher.

Jesus: Two men owed a certain lender a lot of money. One owed 100 weeks' wages, and the other owed 10 weeks' wages. Both men defaulted on their loans, but the lender forgave them both. Here's a question for you: which man will love the lender more?

Simon: Well, I guess it would be the one who was forgiven more.

Jesus: Good answer.

Now Jesus turns around so He's facing the woman, although He's still speaking to Simon.

Jesus: Do you see this woman here? It's kind of funny. I entered your home, and you didn't provide a basin of water so I could wash the road dust from My feet. You didn't give Me a customary kiss of greeting and welcome. You didn't offer Me the common courtesy of providing oil to brighten My face. But this woman has wet My feet with her own tears and washed them with her own hair. She hasn't stopped kissing My feet since I came in. And she has applied perfumed oil to My feet. This woman has been forgiven much, and she is showing much love. But the person who has shown little love shows how little forgiveness he has received.

(to the woman) Your sins are forgiven.

Simon and Friends (*muttering among themselves*): Who does this guy think He is? He has the audacity to claim the authority to forgive sins?

Jesus (*to the woman*): Your faith has liberated you. Go in peace.

Chapter 3

Comparing Wealth

Red-Letter Comparison

But many who are first will be last, and the last first.

—Matthew 19:30

Lesson 1

Putting My Name Tag on the Table

Write out the verse and meditation from page 104:

....

....

....

....

....

....

Record your responses to the questions on page 104:

....

....

....

....

....

....

....

....

....

....

....

....

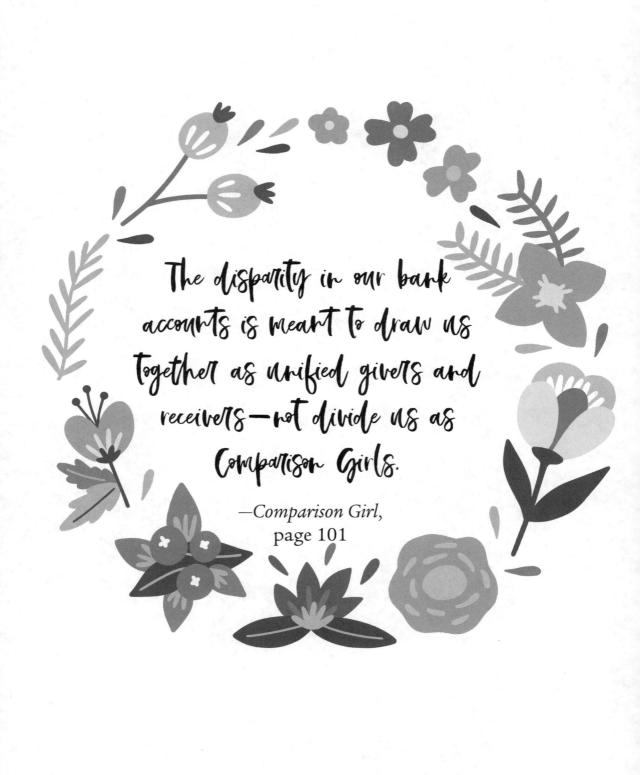

The disparity in our bank accounts is meant to draw us together as unified givers and receivers—not divide us as Comparison Girls.

—Comparison Girl,
page 101

Lesson 2

Camels Are Big; Needles Are Small

Write out the verse and meditation from page 113:

....

....

....

....

....

....

....

....

Record your responses to the questions on page 112:

....

....

....

....

....

....

....

....

....

....

....

....

....

....

living by the Spout

Kara is a twenty-five-year-old single mom who's trying to finish school. She cuts coupons, uses a loaner laptop, and buys secondhand clothes. She's been working with a budget counselor and has a goal of being debt free by the time she's thirty. She's excited about her progress, but sometimes she gets discouraged—like last week when she looked over at someone else's cart in the grocery store.

Kara's cart barely had enough items to cover the bottom of it, and that woman's cart barely had enough room to fit in one more item. Kara thought, *I could never afford all that! Geesh, I'm still living like a broke college kid.*

Tell about a time you looked with frustration over at someone else's "overflowing" grocery cart, closet, yard, or garage? How do you feel after you spend time measuring their lot with yours?

When you focus on the lines of wealth, which of the goals that Jesus has for you are you most distracted from? What is God teaching you about financially living by the spout?

Lesson 3

Rewards Slipping Through My Fingers

Write out the verse and meditation from page 120:

....

....

....

....

....

....

Record your responses to the questions on page 120:

....

....

....

....

....

....

....

....

....

....

....

Our money always tells the true story of how we see God and how we see ourselves.

—*Comparison Girl,*
page 107

Video Session 3

Notes

Bible Study and Discussion

Take some time to study the Bible passages I taught from in the video session. The questions below will help you make observations about the texts (on the next page) and discuss what you're learning. Mark repeated words, correlating ideas, conjunction words, and other notable features. The additional Bible versions on the following pages can aid in your observations as you notice different word choices.

- Contrast the widow in Mark 12:41–44 with the man who wanted more inheritance in Luke 12:13–21. How are they the same? How are their reactions different?

- Mark any words in each passage that denote scarcity (–) and abundance (+). How do the characters in the stories respond to each?

- How does Jesus invite the disciples to compare the widow? How is this comparison different than the type that causes jealousy and strife?

- In Luke 12:15, what does Jesus say to guard against? How does the story help us with that?

- In Luke 12:16–21, when does the story go from being a one-person story to a multiple-person story? How is Jesus inviting us to live in contrast with this?

- In Luke 12:21, what do you think "rich toward God" means? What is it the opposite of?

- Which character do you most relate to in these stories? Why?

Mark 12:41–44

And he sat down opposite the treasury and watched the people putting money into the offering box. Many rich people put in large sums. And a poor widow came and put in two small copper coins, which make a penny. And he called his disciples to him and said to them, "Truly, I say to you, this poor widow has put in more than all those who are contributing to the offering box. For they all contributed out of their abundance, but she out of her poverty has put in everything she had, all she had to live on."

Luke 12:13–21

Someone in the crowd said to him, "Teacher, tell my brother to divide the inheritance with me." But he said to him, "Man, who made me a judge or arbitrator over you?" And he said to them, "Take care, and be on your guard against all covetousness, for one's life does not consist in the abundance of his possessions." And he told them a parable, saying, "The land of a rich man produced plentifully, and he thought to himself, 'What shall I do, for I have nowhere to store my crops?' And he said, 'I will do this: I will tear down my barns and build larger ones, and there I will store all my grain and my goods. And I will say to my soul, "Soul, you have ample goods laid up for many years; relax, eat, drink, be merry."' But God said to him, 'Fool! This night your soul is required of you, and the things you have prepared, whose will they be?' So is the one who lays up treasure for himself and is not rich toward God."

Mark 12:41–44 NIV

Jesus sat down opposite the place where the offerings were put and watched the crowd putting their money into the temple treasury. Many rich people threw in large amounts. But a poor widow came and put in two very small copper coins, worth only a few cents.

Calling his disciples to him, Jesus said, "Truly I tell you, this poor widow has put more into the treasury than all the others. They all gave out of their wealth; but she, out of her poverty, put in everything—all she had to live on."

Mark 12:41–44 NLT

Jesus sat down near the collection box in the Temple and watched as the crowds dropped in their money. Many rich people put in large amounts. Then a poor widow came and dropped in two small coins.

Jesus called his disciples to him and said, "I tell you the truth, this poor widow has given more than all the others who are making contributions. For they gave a tiny part of their surplus, but she, poor as she is, has given everything she had to live on."

Mark 12:41–44 VOICE

Jesus sat down opposite the treasury, where people came to bring their offerings, and He watched as they came and went. Many rich people threw in large sums of money, but a poor widow came and put in only two small coins worth only a fraction of a cent.

Jesus *(calling His disciples together)*: Truly this widow has given a greater gift than any other contribution. All the others gave a little out of their great abundance, but this poor woman has given God everything she has.

Luke 12:13–21 NIV

Someone in the crowd said to him, "Teacher, tell my brother to divide the inheritance with me."

Jesus replied, "Man, who appointed me a judge or an arbiter between you?" Then he said to them, "Watch out! Be on your guard against all kinds of greed; life does not consist in an abundance of possessions."

And he told them this parable: "The ground of a certain rich man yielded an abundant harvest. He thought to himself, 'What shall I do? I have no place to store my crops.'

"Then he said, 'This is what I'll do. I will tear down my barns and build bigger ones, and there I will store my surplus grain. And I'll say to myself, "You have plenty of grain laid up for many years. Take life easy; eat, drink and be merry."'

"But God said to him, 'You fool! This very night your life will be demanded from you. Then who will get what you have prepared for yourself?'

"This is how it will be with whoever stores up things for themselves but is not rich toward God."

Luke 12:13–21 NLT

Then someone called from the crowd, "Teacher, please tell my brother to divide our father's estate with me."

Jesus replied, "Friend, who made me a judge over you to decide such things as that?" Then he said, "Beware! Guard against every kind of greed. Life is not measured by how much you own."

Then he told them a story: "A rich man had a fertile farm that produced fine crops. He said to himself, 'What should I do? I don't have room for all my crops.' Then he said, 'I know! I'll tear down my barns and build bigger ones. Then I'll have room enough to store all my wheat and other goods. And I'll sit back and say to myself, "My friend, you have enough stored away for years to come. Now take it easy! Eat, drink, and be merry!"'

"But God said to him, 'You fool! You will die this very night. Then who will get everything you worked for?'

"Yes, a person is a fool to store up earthly wealth but not have a rich relationship with God."

Luke 12:13–21 VOICE

A person in the crowd got Jesus' attention.

Person in the Crowd: Teacher, intervene and tell my brother to share the family inheritance with me.

Jesus: Since when am I your judge or arbitrator?

Then He used that opportunity to speak to the crowd.

Jesus: You'd better be on your guard against any type of greed, for a person's life is not about having a lot of possessions.

(then, beginning another parable) A wealthy man owned some land that produced a huge harvest. He often thought to himself, "I have a problem here. I don't have anywhere to store all my crops. What should I do? I know! I'll tear down my small barns and build even bigger ones, and then I'll have plenty of storage space for my grain and all my other goods. Then I'll be able to say to myself, 'I have it made! I can relax and take it easy for years! So I'll just sit back, eat, drink, and have a good time!'"

Then God interrupted the man's conversation with himself. "Excuse Me, Mr. Brilliant, but your time has come. Tonight you will die. Now who will enjoy everything you've earned and saved?"

This is how it will be for people who accumulate huge assets for themselves but have no assets in relation to God.

Chapter 4

Comparing Skin-Deep Packaging

Red-Letter Comparison

The greatest among you shall be your servant.

—Matthew 23:11

Lesson 1

A Security Deeper Than Skin

Write out the verse and meditation from page 129:

....
....
....
....
....
....

Record your responses to the questions on pages 128–29:

....
....
....
....
....
....
....
....
....
....
....

A wise woman's most important beauty work is not in front of a mirror; it's before the Lord. As she puts her trust in what God says about her, she builds a foundation which will hold her firm regardless of what storms come.

—*Comparison Girl*,
pages 126–27

Lesson 2

To Be Seen

Write out the verse and meditation from page 138:

....

....

....

....

....

....

....

Record your responses to the questions on pages 137–38:

....

....

....

....

....

....

....

....

....

....

....

Living by the Spout

Carla and her husband decided to move into a finished garage on their property until they could get the old farmhouse they planned to live in renovated. Stuff happened. One delay followed another, and for three years they lived in a garage with no windows, no attached bathroom, and no full-length mirror. The experience was humbling, to put it mildly.

With no full-length mirror available, Carla got used to not seeing herself and not focusing on her appearance nearly as much as she had. She was surprised at how transformative this was. She decided to take her me-free project a step further, and for thirty days, whenever she looked into the mirror, she talked to herself out loud. She told herself what God says is true—even if she wasn't feeling it. She said, "You are fearfully and wonderfully made. God fashioned you. He calls you his child."

How do you approach the mirror? How often do you check yourself? How strong is the magnetic draw of your eyes to your reflection? As you walk past a storefront, how likely are you to check your shape in the reflective glass?

How is the mirror holding you in bondage? How could you challenge yourself toward a new me-free approach to the mirror?

Lesson 3

The Inside of the Cup

Write out the verse and meditation from page 146:

_____

_____

_____

_____

_____

Record your responses to the questions on pages 145–46:

_____

_____

_____

_____

_____

_____

_____

_____

_____

_____

_____

Living by the Spout

In her book **Free of Me**, *Sharon Hodde Miller tells about a time she showed up at church for a women's event dressed up and with her hair and makeup done. In the atrium, she ran into a friend who was a new mom and had barely made it out the door, let alone dressed up. The friend looked at Sharon's outfit, sighed, and said, "Oh, you look cute. You always look cute."*

With compassion for her friend, Sharon writes, "Church should have been a refuge, but instead she was confronted with comparison. All around her were cute, accessorized women whose appearances spotlighted her inadequacy." Of course, we can't solve someone else's insecurity, but Sharon says, "There's a real sense in which women are doing this *to* one another. . . . We contribute to the culture of competition."*

Have you ever felt like this young mom? Where and why?

 How can you help create an environment where other women aren't confronted with comparison when they walk in the door? List several ideas.

---

* Sharon Hodde Miller, *Free of Me: Why Life Is Better When It's Not About You* (Grand Rapids: Baker, 2017), 73–74.

Lesson 4

Whitewashed Tombs

Write out the verse and meditation from page 153:

....

....

....

....

....

....

Record your responses to the questions on page 153:

....

....

....

....

....

....

....

....

....

....

....

Living by the Spout

In video session 4, I share a story from my friend Jen Hand. Jen has an identical twin sister, and back in high school, their school went to an aquarium for a field trip. In one of the dimly lit aquarium rooms, Jen ran into her sister and said, "Hey, how's your day going?" But her sister didn't respond, so she said again, "How are you doing?" Again, her sister didn't respond, so Jen elbowed her sister and said, "Why aren't you talking to me?"

And that's when Jen realized that she wasn't talking to her sister but the reflective glass of a giant fish tank. That story always makes me laugh. Jen always thought that her sister was beautiful. But though they obviously looked pretty similar, when Jen turned her gaze at her own reflection in the mirror, she found no beauty. Nothing to admire or appreciate.

Is it easier to find beauty—like Jen did—in other people than in yourself? Do you critique yourself more harshly than you would someone else?

Consider the response you just journaled. Do you see hints of humility in your words? Or do you see more hints of pride? What do you think Jesus—your creator—would say?

Video Session 4

Notes

Bible Study and Discussion

Take some time to study the Bible passage I taught from in the video session. The questions below will help you make observations about the text (on page 102) and discuss what you're learning. Mark repeated words, correlating ideas, conjunction words, and other notable features. The additional Bible versions on the following pages can aid in your observations as you notice different word choices.

- Mark the repeated words, including *hypocrite*, *secret*, and *reward*.

- What do you learn about each repeated word?

- What is driving the examples of hypocrisy mentioned? How does comparison relate to these motivators? What forms of Comparison Girl hypocrisy are you most prone to?

- Notice that Jesus is not correcting the behaviors but rather the motivations behind the behaviors. Circle each "But when you . . ." phrase, and record Jesus's instructions. How do these new parameters correct the motivation?

- Mark each phrase that begins with "truly." What is Jesus saying is true about these individuals? What might they be believing that is false?

- Contrast the two types of rewards to be received. What does each one require? How is Jesus trying to motivate us?

- Mark the examples of hypocrisy by drawing eyes that are open. List examples of things people do hypocritically to "be seen" today.

- Mark the examples of secrecy by drawing eyes that are closed. How is secrecy different from hypocrisy? How does secrecy improve genuineness?

- What can you apply from this passage to the struggles women face with beauty, measuring up, and appearance?

Matthew 6:1–7, 16–18

"Beware of practicing your righteousness before other people in order to be seen by them, for then you will have no reward from your Father who is in heaven.

"Thus, when you give to the needy, sound no trumpet before you, as the hypocrites do in the synagogues and in the streets, that they may be praised by others. Truly, I say to you, they have received their reward. But when you give to the needy, do not let your left hand know what your right hand is doing, so that your giving may be in secret. And your Father who sees in secret will reward you.

"And when you pray, you must not be like the hypocrites. For they love to stand and pray in the synagogues and at the street corners, that they may be seen by others. Truly, I say to you, they have received their reward. But when you pray, go into your room and shut the door and pray to your Father who is in secret. And your Father who sees in secret will reward you.

"And when you pray, do not heap up empty phrases as the Gentiles do, for they think that they will be heard for their many words. . . .

"And when you fast, do not look gloomy like the hypocrites, for they disfigure their faces that their fasting may be seen by others. Truly, I say to you, they have received their reward. But when you fast, anoint your head and wash your face, that your fasting may not be seen by others but by your Father who is in secret. And your Father who sees in secret will reward you."

Matthew 6:1–7, 16–18 NIV

"Be careful not to practice your righteousness in front of others to be seen by them. If you do, you will have no reward from your Father in heaven.

"So when you give to the needy, do not announce it with trumpets, as the hypocrites do in the synagogues and on the streets, to be honored by others. Truly I tell you, they have received their reward in full. But when you give to the needy, do not let your left hand know what your right hand is doing, so that your giving may be in secret. Then your Father, who sees what is done in secret, will reward you.

"And when you pray, do not be like the hypocrites, for they love to pray standing in the synagogues and on the street corners to be seen by others. Truly I tell you, they have received their reward in full. But when you pray, go into your room, close the door and pray to your Father, who is unseen. Then your Father, who sees what is done in secret, will reward you. And when you pray, do not keep on babbling like pagans, for they think they will be heard because of their many words. . . .

"When you fast, do not look somber as the hypocrites do, for they disfigure their faces to show others they are fasting. Truly I tell you, they have received their reward in full. But when you fast, put oil on your head and wash your face, so that it will not be obvious to others that you are fasting, but only to your Father, who is unseen; and your Father, who sees what is done in secret, will reward you."

Matthew 6:1–7, 16–18 NLT

"Watch out! Don't do your good deeds publicly, to be admired by others, for you will lose the reward from your Father in heaven. When you give to someone in need, don't do as the hypocrites do—blowing trumpets in the synagogues and streets to call attention to their acts of charity! I tell you the truth, they have received all the reward they will ever get. But when you give to someone in need, don't let your left hand know what your right hand is doing. Give your gifts in private, and your Father, who sees everything, will reward you.

"When you pray, don't be like the hypocrites who love to pray publicly on street corners and in the synagogues where everyone can see them. I tell you the truth, that is all the reward they will ever get. But when you pray, go away by yourself, shut the door behind you, and pray to your Father in private. Then your Father, who sees everything, will reward you.

"When you pray, don't babble on and on as the Gentiles do. They think their prayers are answered merely by repeating their words again and again. . . .

"And when you fast, don't make it obvious, as the hypocrites do, for they try to look miserable and disheveled so people will admire them for their fasting. I tell you the truth, that is the only reward they will ever get. But when you fast, comb your hair and wash your face. Then no one will notice that you are fasting, except your Father, who knows what you do in private. And your Father, who sees everything, will reward you."

Matthew 6:1–7, 16–18 VOICE

Jesus: But when you do these righteous acts, do not do them in front of spectators. Don't do them where you can be seen, let alone lauded, by others. If you do, you will have no reward from your Father in heaven. When you give to the poor, do not boast about it, announcing your donations with blaring trumpets as the play actors do. Do not brazenly give your charity in the synagogues and on the streets; indeed, do not give at all if you are giving because you want to be praised by your neighbors. Those people who give in order to reap praise have already received their reward. When you give to the needy, do it in secret—even your left hand should not know what your right hand is doing. Then your Father, who sees in secret, will reward you.

Likewise, when you pray, do not be as hypocrites who love to pray loudly at synagogue or on street corners—their concern is to be seen by men. They have already earned their reward. When you pray, go into a private room, close the door, and pray unseen to your Father who is unseen. Then your Father, who sees in secret, will reward you. And when you pray, do not go on and on, excessively and strangely like the outsiders; they think their verbosity will let them be heard by their deities. . . .

And when you fast, do not look miserable as the actors and hypocrites do when they are fasting—they walk around town putting on airs about their suffering and weakness, complaining about how hungry they are. So everyone will know they are fasting, they don't wash or anoint themselves with oil, pink their cheeks, or wear comfortable shoes. Those who show off their piety, they have already received their reward. When you fast, wash your face and beautify yourself with oil, so no one who looks at you will know about your discipline. Only your Father, who is unseen, will see your fast. And your Father, who sees in secret, will reward you.

Chapter 5

Comparing Our Ministries

Red-Letter Comparison

The last will be first, and the first last.

—Matthew 20:16

Lesson 1

Expecting More

Write out the verse and meditation from page 162:

....

....

....

....

....

....

Record your responses to the questions on page 162:

....

....

....

....

....

....

....

....

....

....

Living by the Spout

April's heart flooded with anxiety when the pastor announced that today was Communion Sunday. Her husband was traveling. Again. Which meant she had no backup to help keep her children—ages eight, six, and four, all lined up in the pew beside her—from being a disruption in church.

April's two boys were poking each other, and her daughter was squirming in her lap. She could feel drops of sweat trickling down her back. And she felt even more frazzled and frustrated when she looked over at the other families sitting contentedly, with the kids nestled between a mom and a dad. Why couldn't *her* husband be here? What was the point of even coming when all she could think about was, *Johnny, please oh please, do not erupt* . . . and, *What is everyone thinking of me right now?*

April wasn't sure whether to be relieved or ashamed when the pastor, after glancing in her direction, made an announcement that the kids would be dismissed *before* Communion this week—so that the parents could have a chance to focus.

In your mothering or some other role, tell about a way you consistently feel frazzled and frustrated like April did—wondering how everyone sees you. Do other families or individuals seem to have an advantage?

Think about what you just wrote. What correlation do you see between your stress and your focus on the lines? How might it restore your confidence and joy to focus on the spout?

Lesson 2

Lumped In as Equals

Write out the verse and meditation from page 170:

....
....
....
....
....
....

Record your responses to the questions on pages 169–70:

....
....
....
....
....
....
....
....
....
....
....
....

Living by the Spout

I was talking with Ash, who serves in worship ministry at our church, about a practice our musicians have before each service. It's not a music practice. Ash says that the musicians come knowing the music. They've practiced. They've prepared. Now, what they need to do is pray.

Before they even warm up, each member of the band chooses a person who will be attending the service and lifts them up in prayer. Ash says this helps quell any nervousness or fear the band members might be experiencing as they prepare to step out in front of a thousand people. I imagine it might also quell any swelling pride. These musicians work to align themselves with Jesus by focusing on the spout, not the measure-up lines.

In what situation do you most feel the eyes of people on you as you serve Jesus? How does your heart respond when you sense people watching you serve?

How can you avoid fixating on the measure-up lines as you serve and turn your focus to the spout instead? Like Ash mentioned, prayer is one way. Can you think of others? What difference could this make in the way you serve?

Lesson 3

Frustrated "Firsts"

Write out the verse and meditation from page 176:

....

....

....

....

....

....

Record your responses to the questions on page 176:

....

....

....

....

....

....

....

....

....

....

....

Not only does our
evil-eyed jealousy
stifle God's glory, it
steals our own joy.

—*Comparison Girl,*
page 174

Lesson 4

Lifting Up "Lasts"

Write out the verse and meditation from page 182:

Record your responses to the questions on pages 181–82:

The amount of talent, wealth, influence, or potential in [my] measuring cup is of no consequence to Jesus, for he can make up for any lack.

—*Comparison Girl,*
page 179

Video Session 5

Notes

Bible Study and Discussion

Take some time to study the Bible passage I taught from in the video session. The questions below will help you make observations about the text (on the next page) and discuss what you're learning. Mark repeated words, correlating ideas, conjunction words, and other notable features. The additional Bible versions on the following pages can aid in your observations as you notice different word choices.

- Mark any comparison and quantity words, such as *little*, *much*, or *more*.

- Highlight the quotes from the master. Which are repeated? Which one is different and why?

- What is the contrast in verse 28? What does this mean?

- What is the contrast in verse 29? What does this mean?

- What do these contrasts teach you about Jesus? What warning is there to apply or advice to be heeded?

- Consider the audience. Jesus is sharing this parable with his disciples. Consider several of the individual disciples. Where do you think they found themselves in the story?

- Keep in mind that the context is Jesus preparing his disciples for his departure. What is Jesus's stated purpose for this parable?

Matthew 25:14–30

"For it will be like a man going on a journey, who called his servants and entrusted to them his property. To one he gave five talents, to another two, to another one, to each according to his ability. Then he went away. He who had received the five talents went at once and traded with them, and he made five talents more. So also he who had the two talents made two talents more. But he who had received the one talent went and dug in the ground and hid his master's money. Now after a long time the master of those servants came and settled accounts with them. And he who had received the five talents came forward, bringing five talents more, saying, 'Master, you delivered to me five talents; here, I have made five talents more.' His master said to him, 'Well done, good and faithful servant. You have been faithful over a little; I will set you over much. Enter into the joy of your master.' And he also who had the two talents came forward, saying, 'Master, you delivered to me two talents; here, I have made two talents more.' His master said to him, 'Well done, good and faithful servant. You have been faithful over a little; I will set you over much. Enter into the joy of your master.' He also who had received the one talent came forward, saying, 'Master, I knew you to be a hard man, reaping where you did not sow, and gathering where you scattered no seed, so I was afraid, and I went and hid your talent in the ground. Here, you have what is yours.' But his master answered him, 'You wicked and slothful servant! You knew that I reap where I have not sown and gather where I scattered no seed? Then you ought to have invested my money with the bankers, and at my coming I should have received what was my own with interest. So take the talent from him and give it to him who has the ten talents. For to everyone who has will more be given, and he will have an abundance. But from the one who has not, even what he has will be taken away. And cast the worthless servant into the outer darkness. In that place there will be weeping and gnashing of teeth.'"

Matthew 25:14–30 NIV

"Again, it will be like a man going on a journey, who called his servants and entrusted his wealth to them. To one he gave five bags of gold, to another two bags, and to another one bag, each according to his ability. Then he went on his journey. The man who had received five bags of gold went at once and put his money to work and gained five bags more. So also, the one with two bags of gold gained two more. But the man who had received one bag went off, dug a hole in the ground and hid his master's money.

"After a long time the master of those servants returned and settled accounts with them. The man who had received five bags of gold brought the other five. 'Master,' he said, 'you entrusted me with five bags of gold. See, I have gained five more.'

"His master replied, 'Well done, good and faithful servant! You have been faithful with a few things; I will put you in charge of many things. Come and share your master's happiness!'

"The man with two bags of gold also came. 'Master,' he said, 'you entrusted me with two bags of gold; see, I have gained two more.'

"His master replied, 'Well done, good and faithful servant! You have been faithful with a few things; I will put you in charge of many things. Come and share your master's happiness!'

"Then the man who had received one bag of gold came. 'Master,' he said, 'I knew that you are a hard man, harvesting where you have not sown and gathering where you have not scattered seed. So I was afraid and went out and hid your gold in the ground. See, here is what belongs to you.'

"His master replied, 'You wicked, lazy servant! So you knew that I harvest where I have not sown and gather where I have not scattered seed? Well then, you should have put my money on deposit with the bankers, so that when I returned I would have received it back with interest.

"'So take the bag of gold from him and give it to the one who has ten bags. For whoever has will be given more, and they will have an abundance. Whoever does not have, even what they have will be taken from them. And throw that worthless servant outside, into the darkness, where there will be weeping and gnashing of teeth.'"

Matthew 25:14–30 NLT

"Again, the Kingdom of Heaven can be illustrated by the story of a man going on a long trip. He called together his servants and entrusted his money to them while he was gone. He gave five bags of silver to one, two bags of silver to another, and one bag of silver to the last—dividing it in proportion to their abilities. He then left on his trip.

"The servant who received the five bags of silver began to invest the money and earned five more. The servant with two bags of silver also went to work and earned two more. But the servant who received the one bag of silver dug a hole in the ground and hid the master's money.

"After a long time their master returned from his trip and called them to give an account of how they had used his money. The servant to whom he had entrusted the five bags of silver came forward with five more and said, 'Master, you gave me five bags of silver to invest, and I have earned five more.'

"The master was full of praise. 'Well done, my good and faithful servant. You have been faithful in handling this small amount, so now I will give you many more responsibilities. Let's celebrate together!'

"The servant who had received the two bags of silver came forward and said, 'Master, you gave me two bags of silver to invest, and I have earned two more.'

"The master said, 'Well done, my good and faithful servant. You have been faithful in handling this small amount, so now I will give you many more responsibilities. Let's celebrate together!'

"Then the servant with the one bag of silver came and said, 'Master, I knew you were a harsh man, harvesting crops you didn't plant and gathering crops you didn't cultivate. I was afraid I would lose your money, so I hid it in the earth. Look, here is your money back.'

"But the master replied, 'You wicked and lazy servant! If you knew I harvested crops I didn't plant and gathered crops I didn't cultivate, why didn't you deposit my money in the bank? At least I could have gotten some interest on it.'

"Then he ordered, 'Take the money from this servant, and give it to the one with the ten bags of silver. To those who use well what they are given, even more will be given, and they will have an abundance. But from those who do nothing, even what little they have will be taken away. Now throw this useless servant into outer darkness, where there will be weeping and gnashing of teeth.'"

Matthew 25:14–30 VOICE

Jesus: This is how it will be. It will be like a landowner who is going on a trip. He instructed his slaves about caring for his property. He gave five talents to one slave, two to the next, and then one talent to the last slave—each according to his ability. Then the man left.

Promptly the man who had been given five talents went out and bartered and sold and turned his five talents into ten. And the one who had received two talents went to the market and turned his two into four. And the slave who had received just one talent? He dug a hole in the ground and buried his master's money there.

Eventually the master came back from his travels, found his slaves, and settled up with them. The slave who had been given five talents came forward and told his master how he'd turned five into ten; then he handed the whole lot over to his master.

> **Master:** Excellent. You've proved yourself not only clever but loyal. You've executed a rather small task masterfully, so now I am going to put you in charge of something larger. But before you go back to work, come join my great feast and celebration.

Then the slave who had been given two talents came forward and told his master how he'd turned two into four, and he handed all four talents to his master.

> **Master:** Excellent. You've proved yourself not only clever but loyal. You've executed a rather small task masterfully, so now I am going to put you in charge of something larger. But before you go back to work, come join my great feast and celebration.

Finally the man who had been given one talent came forward.

Servant: Master, I know you are a hard man, difficult in every way. You can make a healthy sum when others would fail. You profit when other people are doing the work. You grow rich on the backs of others. So I was afraid, dug a hole, and hid the talent in the ground. Here it is. You can have it.

The master was furious.

Master: You are a pathetic excuse for a servant! You have disproved my trust in you and squandered my generosity. You know I always make a profit! You could have at least put this talent in the bank; then I could have earned a little interest on it! Take that one talent away, and give it to the servant who doubled my money from five to ten.

You see, everything was taken away from the man who had nothing, but the man who had something got even more. And as for the slave who made no profit but buried his talent in the ground? His master ordered his slaves to tie him up and throw him outside into the utter darkness where there is miserable mourning and great fear.

Chapter 6

Comparing Status

Red-Letter Comparison

If anyone would be first, he must be last of all and servant of all.

—Mark 9:35

Lesson 1

Equal Opportunity

Write out the verse and meditation from page 189:

....

....

....

....

....

....

....

Record your responses to the questions on page 189:

....

....

....

....

....

....

....

....

....

....

....

Every time we open our arms to someone "small," we receive Jesus and welcome God as our companion.

—*Comparison Girl*, page 189

Lesson 2

Making Myself Small

Write out the verse and meditation from page 195:

....

....

....

....

....

Record your responses to the questions on page 195. Below are the verses for the first question:

> Have this mind among yourselves, which is yours in Christ Jesus, who, though he was in the form of God, did not count equality with God a thing to be grasped, but emptied himself, by taking the form of a servant, being born in the likeness of men. And being found in human form, he humbled himself by becoming obedient to the point of death, even death on a cross. Therefore God has highly exalted him and bestowed on him the name that is above every name, so that at the name of Jesus every knee should bow, in heaven and on earth and under the earth. (Phil. 2:5–10)

....

....

....

....

Living by the Spout

Jill had two preschoolers when she and her husband moved to a new neighborhood, where she quickly connected with several other young moms. The five of them did everything together. But since Jill was the only working mom, she found herself comparing constantly. Was she hurting her kids by not staying home full-time? Was she as good a mom? Since she owned her own business, Jill's schedule was flexible, so she pushed herself to be at all the events the neighborhood moms were planning. The zoo. The moms' day out. The playdates.

One night she and the other moms were out doing a craft that she had no interest in. Jill looked around the table, feeling completely exhausted, and wondered, *What am I doing?* These moms needed to get out of the house, but she needed to be home! She also felt a bit resentful. *Wouldn't it be nice to be rested enough to actually enjoy a night out?* Jill sees now that these other moms didn't have it any easier, but it sure seemed like it at the time.

Are you a mom? Do you compare and worry that you're not keeping up? Do you push yourself to exhaustion or resent other moms who don't seem to be working as hard?

In your mothering, or in some other area where you serve, how does Jesus want you to turn your focus back to serving instead of measuring?

Lesson 3

Seating Requests

Write out the verse and meditation from page 201:

....

....

....

....

....

....

Record your responses to the questions on pages 200–201:

....

....

....

....

....

....

....

....

....

....

....

The sufferings of this
present time are not
worth comparing with
the glory that is to
be revealed to us.

—Romans 8:18

Lesson 4

Mending Circles

Write out the verse and meditation from page 208:

Record your responses to the questions on pages 207–208:

Living by the Spout

On pages 206–207 of **Comparison Girl,** *we read the story of Brittney, whose husband had moved out after twenty-five years of marriage. Remember how Brittney thought about turning back rather than pulling in to the coffee shop to meet her friends? Yet she sensed the Lord saying, "You need people, Brittney. Isolation is not my plan for you."*

Are you, like Brittney, working through some private heartache? How have you been tempted to either break ties with your circle and hide in isolation or hide behind a measure-up facade?

When Brittney called each of her friends to let them know what was really going on, it prompted her friends to be vulnerable and say, "Me too. I have struggles that I also haven't shared." This experience awakened Brittney's desire for authenticity and connection, so she decided to host a Bible study. Instead of breaking ties with her circle, she chose to let her friends be part of her healing.

Whom have you been vulnerable with? How did this invite connectivity? Even if you aren't the official leader, how is God calling you to counterintuitively serve your group in some brave new way? How might God want to use your circle to help heal you? What circle-forming step will you take this week?

Lesson 5

A Broken and Poured-Out King

Write out the verse and meditation from page 215:

....

....

....

....

....

....

Record your responses to the questions on page 215:

....

....

....

....

....

....

....

....

....

....

....

....

....

....

Jesus asked
us to remember
him as a
torn piece of
bread and an
emptied cup.

—*Comparison Girl,*
page 212

Video Session 6

Notes

Bible Study and Discussion

Take some time to study the Bible passage I taught from in the video session. The questions below will help you make observations about the text (on the next page) and discuss what you're learning. Mark repeated words, correlating ideas, conjunction words, and other notable features. The additional Bible versions on the following pages can aid in your observations as you notice different word choices.

- What contrasts do you see between Jesus and Judas?

- Draw an *X* every place Judas is mentioned. What do you learn from Jesus about relating to those who are enemies of God?

- In verses 1–5, mark what Jesus knew, whom he loved, and what he did. How are these related?

- Mark the word *understand*. What do the disciples understand fully? What will they understand later?

- Mark the words *clean* and *wash* in red to represent Jesus's blood.

- Mark the word *feet* in black. Remember that in Middle Eastern cultures, feet are unspeakably dirty. Read the verses, replacing *feet* with sins that seem "unspeakably dirty." Make it personal and silently replace *feet* with your own dirtiest, unspeakable sin. Do you relate to Peter's response in verse 8?

- List the steps Jesus takes in verses 12–13. How is this an example of "littling" but not "belittling" (i.e., Jesus humbled himself, but he didn't deny his position or power)?

- In verses 14–16, circle all the conjunction words and any if-then constructions you find. What do you learn?

John 13:1–17

Now before the Feast of the Passover, when Jesus knew that his hour had come to depart out of this world to the Father, having loved his own who were in the world, he loved them to the end. During supper, when the devil had already put it into the heart of Judas Iscariot, Simon's son, to betray him, Jesus, knowing that the Father had given all things into his hands, and that he had come from God and was going back to God, rose from supper. He laid aside his outer garments, and taking a towel, tied it around his waist. Then he poured water into a basin and began to wash the disciples' feet and to wipe them with the towel that was wrapped around him. He came to Simon Peter, who said to him, "Lord, do you wash my feet?" Jesus answered him, "What I am doing you do not understand now, but afterward you will understand." Peter said to him, "You shall never wash my feet." Jesus answered him, "If I do not wash you, you have no share with me." Simon Peter said to him, "Lord, not my feet only but also my hands and my head!" Jesus said to him, "The one who has bathed does not need to wash, except for his feet, but is completely clean. And you are clean, but not every one of you." For he knew who was to betray him; that was why he said, "Not all of you are clean."

When he had washed their feet and put on his outer garments and resumed his place, he said to them, "Do you understand what I have done to you? You call me Teacher and Lord, and you are right, for so I am. If I then, your Lord and Teacher, have washed your feet, you also ought to wash one another's feet. For I have given you an example, that you also should do just as I have done to you. Truly, truly, I say to you, a servant is not greater than his master, nor is a messenger greater than the one who sent him. If you know these things, blessed are you if you do them."

John 13:1–17 NIV

It was just before the Passover Festival. Jesus knew that the hour had come for him to leave this world and go to the Father. Having loved his own who were in the world, he loved them to the end.

The evening meal was in progress, and the devil had already prompted Judas, the son of Simon Iscariot, to betray Jesus. Jesus knew that the Father had put all things under his power, and that he had come from God and was returning to God; so he got up from the meal, took off his outer clothing, and wrapped a towel around his waist. After that, he poured water into a basin and began to wash his disciples' feet, drying them with the towel that was wrapped around him.

He came to Simon Peter, who said to him, "Lord, are you going to wash my feet?"

Jesus replied, "You do not realize now what I am doing, but later you will understand."

"No," said Peter, "you shall never wash my feet."

Jesus answered, "Unless I wash you, you have no part with me."

"Then, Lord," Simon Peter replied, "not just my feet but my hands and my head as well!"

Jesus answered, "Those who have had a bath need only to wash their feet; their whole body is clean. And you are clean, though not every one of you." For he knew who was going to betray him, and that was why he said not every one was clean.

When he had finished washing their feet, he put on his clothes and returned to his place. "Do you understand what I have done for you?" he asked them. "You call me 'Teacher' and 'Lord,' and rightly so, for that is what I am. Now that I, your Lord and Teacher, have washed your feet, you also should wash one another's feet. I have set you an example that you should do as I have done for you. Very truly I tell you, no servant is greater than his master, nor is a messenger greater than the one who sent him. Now that you know these things, you will be blessed if you do them."

John 13:1–17 NLT

Before the Passover celebration, Jesus knew that his hour had come to leave this world and return to his Father. He had loved his disciples during his ministry on earth, and now he loved them to the very end. It was time for supper, and the devil had already prompted Judas, son of Simon Iscariot, to betray Jesus. Jesus knew that the Father had given him authority over everything and that he had come from God and would return to God. So he got up from the table, took off his robe, wrapped a towel around his waist, and poured water into a basin. Then he began to wash the disciples' feet, drying them with the towel he had around him.

When Jesus came to Simon Peter, Peter said to him, "Lord, are you going to wash my feet?"

Jesus replied, "You don't understand now what I am doing, but someday you will."

"No," Peter protested, "you will never ever wash my feet!"

Jesus replied, "Unless I wash you, you won't belong to me."

Simon Peter exclaimed, "Then wash my hands and head as well, Lord, not just my feet!"

Jesus replied, "A person who has bathed all over does not need to wash, except for the feet, to be entirely clean. And you disciples are clean, but not all of you." For Jesus knew who would betray him. That is what he meant when he said, "Not all of you are clean."

After washing their feet, he put on his robe again and sat down and asked, "Do you understand what I was doing? You call me 'Teacher' and 'Lord,' and you are right, because that's what I am. And since I, your Lord and Teacher, have washed your feet, you ought to wash each other's feet. I have given you an example to follow. Do as I have done to you. I tell you the truth, slaves are not greater than their master. Nor is the messenger more important than the one who sends the message. Now that you know these things, God will bless you for doing them."

John 13:1–17 VOICE

Before the Passover festival began, Jesus was keenly aware that His hour had come to depart from this world and to return to the Father. From beginning to end, Jesus' days were marked by His love for His people. Before Jesus and His disciples gathered for dinner, the adversary filled Judas Iscariot's heart with plans of deceit and betrayal. Jesus, knowing that He had come from God and was going away to God, stood up from dinner and removed His outer garments. He then wrapped Himself in a towel, poured water in a basin, and began to wash the feet of the disciples, drying them with His towel.

Simon Peter *(as Jesus approaches)***:** Lord, are You going to wash my feet?

Jesus: Peter, you don't realize what I am doing, but you will understand later.

Peter: You will not wash my feet, now or ever!

Jesus: If I don't wash you, you will have nothing to do with Me.

Peter: Then wash me but don't stop with my feet. Cleanse my hands and head as well.

Jesus: Listen, anyone who has bathed is clean all over except for the feet. But I tell you this, not all of you are clean.

He knew the one with plans of betraying Him, which is why He said, "not all of you are clean." After washing their feet and picking up His garments, He reclined at the table again.

Jesus: Do you understand what I have done to you? You call Me Teacher and Lord, and truly, that is who I am. So if your Lord and Teacher washes your feet, then you should wash one another's feet. I am your example; keep doing what I do. I tell you the truth: a servant is not greater than the master. Those who are sent are not greater than the one who sends them. If you know these things, and if you put them into practice, you will find happiness.

Conclusion

"Lord, What About Her?"

Read pages 217–19 in *Comparison Girl* and John 21:1–22, then put yourself in the scene with Jesus. You've just had breakfast on the beach with a group of disciples, and now Jesus invites you to take a walk. Just you and him. There are things you need to talk about. Jesus has exciting work for you to do. The kingdom doors have swung open wide, and you're invited to participate! And to invite others in! Your specific assignments will be tied to whatever is in your measuring cup.

What kingdom-worthy measuring cup contents have you become more aware of? Record the specific ways that you sense Jesus inviting you to pour yourself out. Declare to him your willingness to risk it all for the sake of the kingdom.

As you walk along the shore with Jesus, you can't help but glance back and notice there's somebody trailing behind. It's that person you're most tempted to compare yourself with. As Jesus shares about what's ahead, you interrupt and say, "Lord, what about her?"

Write down the ways you're still tempted to measure yourself against others, even after working through these lessons of Jesus on me-free living:

After hearing your question, Jesus stops and puts his hands on your shoulders. Looking deep into your eyes, he says in a firm but soft tone, "What's that to you? You follow me."

Jesus has been so patient with you, but you know it's time. He wants you to be done with the measure-up mindset of the world. Instead of listening to the world or your enemy, Jesus wants you to listen for *his* voice and follow *him*.

As you think back through these lessons with Jesus, where have you most found yourself in the pages of your Bible? Do you see yourself in one of the stories he told? Or in one of the conversations he had with the Pharisees, the disciples, or the tax collectors?

Which of Jesus's red-letter comparisons—offered to the people he met on the roads of Galilee—do you think will provide the most guidance for you as you navigate the path ahead? If you stumble or become tempted to turn your eyes back to the lines, how might these red-letter comparisons anchor you? How will they clear away the measure-up smog of this world and restore your confidence and joy?

Respond to these verses written by Paul—a follower of Jesus who poured out everything he had for the sake of the kingdom. How do they motivate you to live by the spout?

> For this light momentary affliction is preparing for us an eternal weight of glory *beyond all comparison*, as we look not to the things that are seen but to the things that are unseen. For the things that are seen are transient, but the things that are unseen are eternal. (2 Cor. 4:17–18, emphasis added)

Does Your Heart Crave Control?

Don't miss Shannon's best-selling first book!

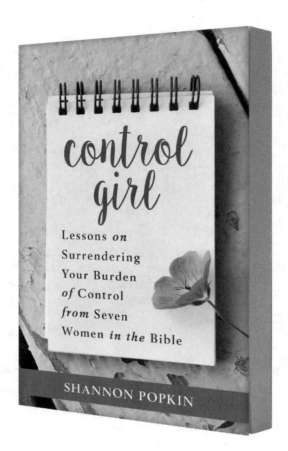

"*Control Girl* is a penetrating look at how selfishness and self-protectiveness wreck lives—and why surrender and trust are God's life-giving pathways to true freedom and joy."
—**Nancy DeMoss Wolgemuth**, author and *Revive Our Hearts* teacher and host

"In the style of Liz Curtis Higgs, *Control Girl* is an easy and entertaining read, yet Shannon packs a punch where we so need it!"
—**Dee Brestin**, author of *Idol Lies*

The perfect pack for group study

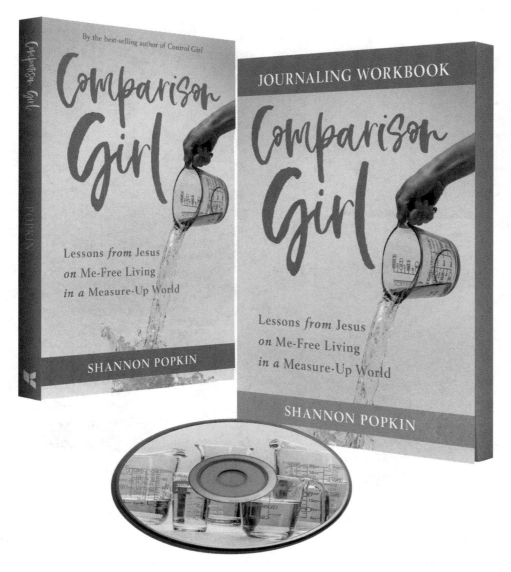

Whether you're inspired to lead or just want to learn how to resist the comparison trap with the support of other women, this complete Bible study kit is perfect to help any group seek the way of Jesus together!

But wait, there's more!

From freebies to video courses to more wise words, ShannonPopkin.com has everything you need to inspire you to live like God's Word is true!

Shannon invites you to join her in her passion for Jesus—and to continue your journey to become the woman you were designed to be. Read her blog, follow her on Instagram, or drop her a note to let her know how God has worked in your life.

Visit ShannonPopkin.com today!